The Miracles and Parables of Jesus:

  The Four Gospel Parallel Accounts

CreateSpace

Nonfiction / Reference / Publishing

First Edition (May 2011)

ISBN-13: 978-1463553913

Table of Contents   page

Part I: The Miracles Of Jesus

Part II: The Parables of Jesus

TEACHING PARABLES ABOUT THE KINGDOM OF GOD

TEACHING PARABLES ABOUT SERVICE AND OBEDIENCE

TEACHING PARABLES ABOUT PRAYER

TEACHING PARABLES ABOUT NEIGHBORS

TEACHING PARABLES ABOUT HUMILITY

TEACHING PARABLES ABOUT WEALTH

Part I: The Miracles Of Jesus

1. FIVE THOUSAND PEOPLE ARE FED

Matthew14:15-21

[15]As evening approached, the disciples came to him and said, "This is a remote place, and it's already getting late. Send the crowds away, so they can go to the villages and buy themselves some food."

[16]Jesus replied, "They do not need to go away. You give them something to eat."

[17]"We have here only five loaves of bread and two fish," they answered.

[18]"Bring them here to me," he said. [19]And he directed the people to sit down on the grass. Taking the five loaves and the two fish and looking up to heaven, he gave thanks and broke the loaves. Then he gave them to the disciples, and the disciples gave them to the people. [20]They all ate and were satisfied, and the disciples picked up twelve basketfuls of broken pieces that were left over. [21]The number of those who ate was about five thousand men, besides women and children. (NIV)

Mark 6:35-44

35 By this time it was late in the day, so his disciples came to him. "This is a remote place," they said, "and it's already very late. 36 Send the people away so that they can go to the surrounding countryside and villages and buy themselves something to eat."

37 But he answered, "You give them something to eat."

They said to him, "That would take more than half a year's wages! Are we to go and spend that much on bread and give it to them to eat?"

38 "How many loaves do you have?" he asked. "Go and see."

When they found out, they said, "Five—and two fish."

39 Then Jesus directed them to have all the people sit down in groups on the green grass. 40 So they sat down in groups of hundreds and fifties. 41 Taking the five loaves and the two fish and looking up to heaven, he gave thanks and broke the loaves. Then he gave them to his disciples to distribute to the people. He also divided the two fish among them all. 42 They all ate and were satisfied, 43 and the disciples picked up twelve basketfuls of broken pieces of bread and fish. 44 The number of the men who had eaten was five thousand. (NIV)

Luke 9:12-17

[12] Late in the afternoon the Twelve came to him and said, "Send the crowd away so they can go to the surrounding villages and countryside and find food and lodging, because we are in a remote place here."

[13] He replied, "You give them something to eat."

They answered, "We have only five loaves of bread and two fish—unless we go and buy food for all this crowd." [14] (About five thousand men were there.)

But he said to his disciples, "Have them sit down in groups of about fifty each." [15] The disciples did so, and everyone sat down. [16] Taking the five loaves and the two fish and looking up to heaven, he gave thanks and broke them. Then he gave them to the disciples to distribute to the people. [17] They all ate and were satisfied, and the disciples picked up twelve basketfuls of broken pieces that were left over. (NIV)

John 6:5-14

[5] When Jesus looked up and saw a great crowd coming toward him, he said to Philip, "Where shall we buy bread for these people to eat?" [6] He asked this only to test him, for he already had in mind what he was going to do.

[7] Philip answered him, "It would take more than half a year's wages to buy enough bread for each one to have a bite!"

[8] Another of his disciples, Andrew, Simon Peter's brother, spoke up, [9] "Here is a boy with five small barley loaves and two small fish, but how far will they go among so many?"

[10] Jesus said, "Have the people sit down." There was plenty of grass in that place, and they sat down (about five thousand men were there). [11] Jesus then took the loaves, gave thanks, and distributed to those who were seated as much as they wanted. He did the same with the fish.

[12] When they had all had enough to eat, he said to his disciples, "Gather the pieces that are left over. Let nothing be wasted." [13] So they

gathered them and filled twelve baskets with the pieces of the five barley loaves left over by those who had eaten.

[14] After the people saw the sign Jesus performed, they began to say, "Surely this is the Prophet who is to come into the world." (NIV)

2. CALMING THE STORM

Matthew 8:23-27

23 Then he got into the boat and his disciples followed him. 24 Suddenly a furious storm came up on the lake, so that the waves swept over the boat. But Jesus was sleeping. 25 The disciples went and woke him, saying, "Lord, save us! We're going to drown!"

26 He replied, "You of little faith, why are you so afraid?" Then he got up and rebuked the winds and the waves, and it was completely calm.

27 The men were amazed and asked, "What kind of man is this? Even the winds and the waves obey him!" (NIV)

Mark 4:35-41

35 That day when evening came, he said to his disciples, "Let us go over to the other side."

36 Leaving the crowd behind, they took him along, just as he was, in the boat. There were also other boats with him. 37 A furious squall came up, and the waves broke over the boat, so that it was nearly swamped.

38 Jesus was in the stern, sleeping on a cushion. The disciples woke him and said to him, "Teacher, don't you care if we drown?"

39 He got up, rebuked the wind and said to the waves, "Quiet! Be still!" Then the wind died down and it was completely calm.

40 He said to his disciples, "Why are you so afraid? Do you still have no faith?"

41 They were terrified and asked each other, "Who is this? Even the wind and the waves obey him!" (NIV)

10

Luke 8:22-25

[22] One day Jesus said to his disciples, "Let us go over to the other side of the lake." So they got into a boat and set out. [23] As they sailed, he fell asleep. A squall came down on the lake, so that the boat was being swamped, and they were in great danger.

[24] The disciples went and woke him, saying, "Master, Master, we're going to drown!"

He got up and rebuked the wind and the raging waters; the storm subsided, and all was calm. [25] "Where is your faith?" he asked his disciples. (NIV)

3. DEMONS SENT INTO THE PIGS

Matthew 8:28-34

Mark 5:1-20

28 When he arrived at the other side in the region of the Gadarenes, two demon-possessed men coming from the tombs met him. They were so violent that no one could pass that way. 29 "What do you want with us, Son of God?" they shouted. "Have you come here to torture us before the appointed time?"

30 Some distance from them a large herd of pigs was feeding. 31 The demons begged Jesus, "If you drive us out, send us into the herd of pigs."

32 He said to them, "Go!" So they came out and went into the pigs, and the whole herd rushed down the steep bank into the lake and died in the water. 33 Those tending the pigs ran off, went into the town and reported all this, including what had happened to the demon-possessed men. 34 Then the whole town went out to meet Jesus. And when they saw him, they pleaded with him to leave their region. (NIV)

1 They went across the lake to the region of the Gerasenes. 2 When Jesus got out of the boat, a man with an impure spirit came from the tombs to meet him. 3 This man lived in the tombs, and no one could bind him anymore, not even with a chain. 4 For he had often been chained hand and foot, but he tore the chains apart and broke the irons on his feet. No one was strong enough to subdue him. 5 Night and day among the tombs and in the hills he would cry out and cut himself with stones.

6 When he saw Jesus from a distance, he ran and fell on his knees in front of him. 7 He shouted at the top of his voice, "What do you want with me, Jesus, Son of the Most High God? In God's name don't torture me!" 8 For Jesus had said to him, "Come out of this man, you impure spirit!"

9 Then Jesus asked him, "What is your name?"

"My name is Legion," he replied, "for we are many." 10 And he begged Jesus again and again not to send them out of the area.

[11] A large herd of pigs was feeding on the nearby hillside. [12] The demons begged Jesus, "Send us among the pigs; allow us to go into them." [13] He gave them permission, and the impure spirits came out and went into the pigs. The herd, about two thousand in number, rushed down the steep bank into the lake and were drowned.

[14] Those tending the pigs ran off and reported this in the town and countryside, and the people went out to see what had happened. [15] When they came to Jesus, they saw the man who had been possessed by the legion of demons, sitting there, dressed and in his right mind; and they were afraid. [16] Those who had seen it told the people what had happened to the demon-possessed man—and told about the pigs as well. [17] Then the people began to plead with Jesus to leave their region.

[18] As Jesus was getting into the boat, the man who had been demon-possessed begged to go with him. [19] Jesus did not let him, but said, "Go home to your own people and tell them how much the Lord has done for you, and how he has had mercy on you." [20] So the man went away and began to tell in the Decapolis[b] how much Jesus had done for him. And all the people were amazed. (NIV)

Luke 8:26-39

26 They sailed to the region of the Gerasenes,[b] which is across the lake from Galilee. 27 When Jesus stepped ashore, he was met by a demon-possessed man from the town. For a long time this man had not worn clothes or lived in a house, but had lived in the tombs. 28 When he saw Jesus, he cried out and fell at his feet, shouting at the top of his voice, "What do you want with me, Jesus, Son of the Most High God? I beg you, don't torture me!" 29 For Jesus had commanded the impure spirit to come out of the man. Many times it had seized him, and though he was chained hand and foot and kept under guard, he had broken his chains and had been driven by the demon into solitary places.

30 Jesus asked him, "What is your name?"

"Legion," he replied, because many demons had gone into him. 31 And they begged Jesus repeatedly not to order them to go into the Abyss.

32 A large herd of pigs was feeding there on the hillside. The demons begged Jesus to let them go into the pigs, and he gave them permission. 33 When the demons came out of the man, they went into the pigs, and the herd rushed down the steep bank into the lake and was drowned.

34 When those tending the pigs saw what had happened, they ran off and reported this in the town and countryside, 35 and the people went out to see what had happened. When they came to Jesus, they found the man from whom the demons had gone out, sitting at Jesus' feet, dressed and in his right mind; and they were afraid. 36 Those who had seen it told the people how the demon-possessed man had been cured. 37 Then all the people of the region of the Gerasenes asked Jesus to leave them, because they were overcome with fear. So he got into the boat and left.

38 The man from whom the demons had gone out begged to go with him, but Jesus sent him away, saying, 39 "Return home and tell how

much God has done for you." So the man went away and told all over town how much Jesus had done for him. (NIV)

"Good Morning Lord" By Barry L. Barnes

4. JAIRUS'S DAUGHTER RAISED

Matthew 9:18,19,23-26

¹⁸ While he was saying this, a synagogue leader came and knelt before him and said, "My daughter has just died. But come and put your hand on her, and she will live." ¹⁹ Jesus got up and went with him, and so did his disciples.

²³ When Jesus entered the synagogue leader's house and saw the noisy crowd and people playing pipes, ²⁴ he said, "Go away. The girl is not dead but asleep." But they laughed at him. ²⁵ After the crowd had been put outside, he went in and took the girl by the hand, and she got up. ²⁶ News of this spread through all that region. (NIV)

Mark 5:22-24, 35-43

²² Then one of the synagogue leaders, named Jairus, came, and when he saw Jesus, he fell at his feet. ²³ He pleaded earnestly with him, "My little daughter is dying. Please come and put your hands on her so that she will be healed and live." ²⁴ So Jesus went with him. A large crowd followed and pressed around him.

³⁵ While Jesus was still speaking, some people came from the house of Jairus, the synagogue leader. "Your daughter is dead," they said. "Why bother the teacher anymore?"

³⁶ Overhearing what they said, Jesus told him, "Don't be afraid; just believe."

³⁷ He did not let anyone follow him except Peter, James and John the brother of James. ³⁸ When they came to the home of the synagogue leader, Jesus saw a commotion, with people crying and wailing loudly. ³⁹ He went in and said to them, "Why all this commotion and wailing?

16

The child is not dead but asleep." [40] But they laughed at him.

After he put them all out, he took the child's father and mother and the disciples who were with him, and went in where the child was. [41] He took her by the hand and said to her, *"Talitha koum!"* (which means "Little girl, I say to you, get up!"). [42] Immediately the girl stood up and began to walk around (she was twelve years old). At this they were completely astonished. [43] He gave strict orders not to let anyone know about this, and told them to give her something to eat. (NIV)

Luke 8:41, 42, 49-56

[41]Then a man named Jairus, a ruler of the synagogue, came and fell at Jesus' feet, pleading with him to come to his house [42]because his only daughter, a girl of about twelve, was dying.

[49]While Jesus was still speaking, someone came from the house of Jairus, the synagogue ruler. "Your daughter is dead," he said. "Don't bother the teacher any more."

[50]Hearing this, Jesus said to Jairus, "Don't be afraid; just believe, and she will be healed."

[51]When he arrived at the house of Jairus, he did not let anyone go in with him except Peter, John and James, and the child's father and mother. [52]Meanwhile, all the people were wailing and mourning for her. "Stop wailing," Jesus said. "She is not dead but asleep."

[53]They laughed at him, knowing that she was dead. [54]But he took her by the hand and said, "My child, get up!" [55]Her spirit returned, and at once she stood up. Then Jesus told them to give her something to eat. [56]Her parents were astonished, but he ordered them not to tell anyone what had happened. (NIV)

5. A SICK WOMAN IS HEALED

Matthew 9:20-22

²⁰ Just then a woman who had been subject to bleeding for twelve years came up behind him and touched the edge of his cloak. ²¹ She said to herself, "If I only touch his cloak, I will be healed."

²² Jesus turned and saw her. "Take heart, daughter," he said, "your faith has healed you." And the woman was healed at that moment. (NIV)

Mark 5:25-34

A large crowd followed and pressed around him. ²⁵And a woman was there who had been subject to bleeding for twelve years. ²⁶She had suffered a great deal under the care of many doctors and had spent all she had, yet instead of getting better she grew worse. ²⁷When she heard about Jesus, she came up behind him in the crowd and touched his cloak, ²⁸because she thought, "If I just touch his clothes, I will be healed." ²⁹Immediately her bleeding stopped and she felt in her body that she was freed from her suffering.

³⁰At once Jesus realized that power had gone out from him. He turned around in the crowd and asked, "Who touched my clothes?"

³¹"You see the people crowding against you," his disciples answered, "and yet you can ask, 'Who touched me?' "

³²But Jesus kept looking around to see who had done it. ³³Then the woman, knowing what had happened to her, came and fell at his feet and, trembling with fear, told him the whole truth.

[34]He said to her, "Daughter, your faith has healed you. Go in peace and be freed from your suffering." (NIV)

Luke 8:43-48

[43] And a woman was there who had been subject to bleeding for twelve years, but no one could heal her. [44] She came up behind him and touched the edge of his cloak, and immediately her bleeding stopped.

[45] "Who touched me?" Jesus asked.

When they all denied it, Peter said, "Master, the people are crowding and pressing against you."

[46] But Jesus said, "Someone touched me; I know that power has gone out from me."

[47] Then the woman, seeing that she could not go unnoticed, came trembling and fell at his feet. In the presence of all the people, she told why she had touched him and how she had been instantly healed. [48] Then he said to her, "Daughter, your faith has healed you. Go in peace." (NIV)

6. JESUS HEALS A PARALYTIC

Matthew 9:1-8

[1]Jesus stepped into a boat, crossed over and came to his own town. [2]Some men brought to him a paralytic, lying on a mat. When Jesus saw their faith, he said to the paralytic, "Take heart, son; your sins are forgiven."

[3]At this, some of the teachers of the law said to themselves, "This fellow is blaspheming!"

[4]Knowing their thoughts, Jesus said, "Why do you entertain evil thoughts in your hearts? [5]Which is easier: to say, 'Your sins are forgiven,' or to say, 'Get up and walk'? [6]But so that you may know that the Son of Man has authority on earth to forgive sins...." Then he said to the paralytic, "Get up, take your mat and go home." [7]And the man got up and went home. [8]When the crowd saw this, they were filled with awe; and they praised God, who had given such authority to men. (NIV)

Mark 2:1-12

[1]A few days later, when Jesus again entered Capernaum, the people heard that he had come home. [2]So many gathered that there was no room left, not even outside the door, and he preached the word to them. [3]Some men came, bringing to him a paralytic, carried by four of them. [4]Since they could not get him to Jesus because of the crowd, they made an opening in the roof above Jesus and, after digging through it, lowered the mat the paralyzed man was lying on. [5]When Jesus saw their faith, he said to the paralytic, "Son, your sins are forgiven."

[6]Now some teachers of the law were sitting there, thinking to themselves, [7]"Why does this fellow talk like that? He's blaspheming! Who can forgive sins but God alone?"

[8]Immediately Jesus knew in his spirit that this was what they were thinking in their hearts, and he said to them, "Why are you thinking these things? [9]Which is easier: to say to the paralytic, 'Your sins are forgiven,' or to say, 'Get up, take your mat and walk'? [10]But that you may know that the Son of Man has authority on earth to

forgive sins . . . ." He said to the paralytic, [11]"I tell you, get up, take your mat and go home." [12]He got up, took his mat and walked out in full view of them all. This amazed everyone and they praised God, saying, "We have never seen anything like this!" (NIV)

Luke 5:17-26

[17]One day as he was teaching, Pharisees and teachers of the law, who had come from every village of Galilee and from Judea and Jerusalem, were sitting there. And the power of the Lord was present for him to heal the sick. [18]Some men came carrying a paralytic on a mat and tried to take him into the house to lay him before Jesus. [19]When they could not find a way to do this because of the crowd, they went up on the roof and lowered him on his mat through the tiles into the middle of the crowd, right in front of Jesus.

[20]When Jesus saw their faith, he said, "Friend, your sins are forgiven."

[21]The Pharisees and the teachers of the law began thinking to themselves, "Who is this fellow who speaks blasphemy? Who can forgive sins but God alone?"

[22]Jesus knew what they were thinking and asked, "Why are you thinking these things in your hearts? [23]Which is easier: to say, 'Your sins are forgiven,' or to say, 'Get up and walk'? [24]But that you may know that the Son of Man has authority on earth to forgive sins...." He said to the paralyzed man, "I tell you, get up, take your mat and go home." [25]Immediately he stood up in front of them, took what he had been lying on and went home praising God. [26]Everyone was amazed and gave praise to God. They were filled with awe and said, "We have seen remarkable things today." (NIV)

7. A LEPER IS HEALED AT GENNESARET

Matthew 8:1-4

[1]When he came down from the mountainside, large crowds followed him. [2]A man with leprosy came and knelt before him and said, "Lord, if you are willing, you can make me clean."

[3]Jesus reached out his hand and touched the man. "I am willing," he said. "Be clean!" Immediately he was cured of his leprosy. [4]Then Jesus said to him, "See that you don't tell anyone. But go, show yourself to the priest and offer the gift Moses commanded, as a testimony to them." (NIV)

Mark 1:40-45

[40]A man with leprosy came to him and begged him on his knees, "If you are willing, you can make me clean."

[41]Filled with compassion, Jesus reached out his hand and touched the man. "I am willing," he said. "Be clean!" [42]Immediately the leprosy left him and he was cured.

[43]Jesus sent him away at once with a strong warning: [44]"See that you don't tell this to anyone. But go, show yourself to the priest and offer the sacrifices that Moses commanded for your cleansing, as a testimony to them." [45]Instead he went out and began to talk freely, spreading the news. As a result, Jesus could no longer enter a town openly but stayed outside in lonely places. Yet the people still came to him from everywhere. (NIV)

Luke 5:12-15

[12]While Jesus was in one of the towns, a man came along who was covered with leprosy.[a] When he saw Jesus, he fell with his face to the ground and begged him, "Lord, if you are willing, you can make me clean."

[13]Jesus reached out his hand and touched the man. "I am willing," he said. "Be clean!" And immediately the leprosy left him.

[14]Then Jesus ordered him, "Don't tell anyone, but go, show yourself to the priest and offer the sacrifices that Moses commanded for your cleansing, as a testimony to them."

[15]Yet the news about him spread all the more, so that crowds of people came to hear him and to be healed of their sicknesses. (NIV)

8. PETER'S MOTHER-IN-LAW HEALED

Matthew 8:14-17

[14]When Jesus came into Peter's house, he saw Peter's mother-in-law lying in bed with a fever. [15]He touched her hand and the fever left her, and she got up and began to wait on him.

[16]When evening came, many who were demon-possessed were brought to him, and he drove out the spirits with a word and healed all the sick. [17]This was to fulfill what was spoken through the prophet Isaiah:

"He took up our infirmities
  and carried our diseases." (NIV)

Mark 1:29-31

[29]As soon as they left the synagogue, they went with James and John to the home of Simon and Andrew. [30]Simon's mother-in-law was in bed with a fever, and they told Jesus about her. [31]So he went to her, took her hand and helped her up. The fever left her and she began to wait on them. (NIV)

Luke 4:38, 39

38 Jesus left the synagogue and went to the home of Simon. Now Simon's mother-in-law was suffering from a high fever, and they asked Jesus to help her. 39 So he bent over her and rebuked the fever, and it left her. She got up at once and began to wait on them. (NIV)

9. A SHRIVELED HAND IS RESTORED

Matthew 12:9-13

[9] Now when He had departed from there, He went into their synagogue. [10] And behold, there was a man who had a withered hand. And they asked Him, saying, "Is it lawful to heal on the Sabbath?"—that they might accuse Him. [11] Then He said to them, "What man is there among you who has one sheep, and if it falls into a pit on the Sabbath, will not lay hold of it and lift *it* out? [12] Of how much more value then is a man than a sheep? Therefore it is lawful to do good on the Sabbath." [13] Then He said to the man, "Stretch out your hand." And he stretched *it* out, and it was restored as whole as the other. (NKJV)

Mark 3:1-5

[1] And He entered the synagogue again, and a man was there who had a withered hand. [2] So they watched Him closely, whether He would heal him on the Sabbath, so that they might accuse Him. [3] And He said to the man who had the withered hand, "Step forward." [4] Then He said to them, "Is it lawful on the Sabbath to do good or to do evil, to save life or to kill?" But they kept silent. [5] And when He had looked around at them with anger, being grieved by the hardness of their hearts, He said to the man, "Stretch out your hand." And he stretched *it* out, and his hand was restored as whole as the other. (NKJV)

Luke 6:6-11

[6] Now it happened on another Sabbath, also, that He entered the synagogue and taught. And a man was there whose right hand was withered. [7] So the scribes and Pharisees watched Him closely, whether He would heal on the Sabbath, that they might find an accusation against Him. [8] But He knew their thoughts, and said to the man who had the withered hand, "Arise and stand here." And he arose and stood. [9] Then Jesus said to them, "I will ask you one thing: Is it lawful on the Sabbath to do good or to do evil, to save life or to destroy?" [10] And when He had looked around at them all, He said to the man, "Stretch out your hand." And he did so, and his hand was restored as whole as the other.[11] But they were filled with rage, and discussed with one another what they might do to Jesus. (NKJV)

10. A BOY WITH AN EVIL SPIRIT IS HEALED

Matthew 17:14-21

Mark 9:14-29

[14] And when they had come to the multitude, a man came to Him, kneeling down to Him and saying, [15] "Lord, have mercy on my son, for he is an epileptic and suffers severely; for he often falls into the fire and often into the water. [16] So I brought him to Your disciples, but they could not cure him."

[17] Then Jesus answered and said, "O faithless and perverse generation, how long shall I be with you? How long shall I bear with you? Bring him here to Me." [18] And Jesus rebuked the demon, and it came out of him; and the child was cured from that very hour.

[19] Then the disciples came to Jesus privately and said, "Why could we not cast it out?"

[20] So Jesus said to them, "Because of your unbelief; for assuredly, I say to you, if you have faith as a mustard seed, you will say to this mountain, 'Move from here to there,' and it will move; and nothing will be impossible for you. [21] However, this kind does not go out except by prayer and fasting." (NKJV)

[14] And when He came to the disciples, He saw a great multitude around them, and scribes disputing with them. [15] Immediately, when they saw Him, all the people were greatly amazed, and running to *Him,* greeted Him. [16] And He asked the scribes, "What are you discussing with them?"

[17] Then one of the crowd answered and said, "Teacher, I brought You my son, who has a mute spirit. [18] And wherever it seizes him, it throws him down; he foams at the mouth, gnashes his teeth, and becomes rigid. So I spoke to Your disciples, that they should cast it out, but they could not."

[19] He answered him and said, "O faithless generation, how long shall I be with you? How long shall I bear with you? Bring him to Me." [20] Then they brought him to Him. And when he saw Him, immediately the spirit convulsed him, and he fell on the ground and wallowed, foaming at the mouth.

[21] So He asked his father, "How long has this been happening to him?"

And he said, "From childhood. [22] And often he

has thrown him both into the fire and into the water to destroy him. But if You can do anything, have compassion on us and help us."

23 Jesus said to him, "If you can believe, all things *are* possible to him who believes."

24 Immediately the father of the child cried out and said with tears, "Lord, I believe; help my unbelief!"

25 When Jesus saw that the people came running together, He rebuked the unclean spirit, saying to it, "Deaf and dumb spirit, I command you, come out of him and enter him no more!" 26 Then *the spirit* cried out, convulsed him greatly, and came out of him. And he became as one dead, so that many said, "He is dead." 27 But Jesus took him by the hand and lifted him up, and he arose.

28 And when He had come into the house, His disciples asked Him privately, "Why could we not cast it out?"

29 So He said to them, "This kind can come out by nothing but prayer and fasting." (NKJV)

Luke 9:37-42

37 Now it happened on the next day, when they had come down from the mountain, that a great multitude met Him. 38 Suddenly a man from the multitude cried out, saying, "Teacher, I implore You, look on my son, for he is my only child. 39 And behold, a spirit seizes him, and he suddenly cries out; it convulses him so that he foams *at the mouth;* and it departs from him with great difficulty, bruising him. 40 So I implored Your disciples to cast it out, but they could not."

41 Then Jesus answered and said, "O faithless and perverse generation, how long shall I be with you and bear with you? Bring your son here." 42 And as he was still coming, the demon threw him down and convulsed *him.* Then Jesus rebuked the unclean spirit, healed the child, and gave him back to his father. (NKJV)

11. JESUS WALKS ON THE WATER

Matthew 14:22-33

[22] Immediately Jesus made His disciples get into the boat and go before Him to the other side, while He sent the multitudes away. [23] And when He had sent the multitudes away, He went up on the mountain by Himself to pray. Now when evening came, He was alone there. [24] But the boat was now in the middle of the sea, tossed by the waves, for the wind was contrary.

[25] Now in the fourth watch of the night Jesus went to them, walking on the sea. [26] And when the disciples saw Him walking on the sea, they were troubled, saying, "It is a ghost!" And they cried out for fear.

[27] But immediately Jesus spoke to them, saying, "Be of good cheer! It is I; do not be afraid."

[28] And Peter answered Him and said, "Lord, if it is You, command me to come to You on the water."

[29] So He said, "Come." And when Peter had come down out of the boat, he walked on the water to go to Jesus. [30] But when he saw that the wind *was* boisterous, he was afraid; and beginning to sink he cried out, saying, "Lord, save me!"

[31] And immediately Jesus stretched out *His* hand and caught him, and said to him, "O you of little faith, why did you doubt?" [32] And when they got into the boat, the wind ceased.

[33] Then those who were in the boat came and worshiped Him, saying, "Truly You are the Son of God." (NKJV)

Mark 6:45-52

[45] Immediately He made His disciples get into the boat and go before Him to the other side, to Bethsaida, while He sent the multitude away. [46] And when He had sent them away, He departed to the mountain to pray. [47] Now when evening came, the boat was in the middle of the sea; and He *was* alone on the land. [48] Then He saw them straining at rowing, for the wind was against them. Now about the fourth watch of the night He came to them, walking on the sea, and would have passed them by. [49] And when they saw Him walking on the sea, they supposed it was a ghost, and cried out; [50] for they all saw Him and were troubled. But immediately He talked with them and said to them, "Be of good cheer! It is I; do not be afraid." [51] Then He went up into the boat to them, and the wind ceased. And they were greatly amazed in themselves beyond measure, and marveled. [52] For they had not understood about the loaves, because their heart was hardened. (NKJV)

John 6:16-21

[16] Now when evening came, His disciples went down to the sea, [17] got into the boat, and went over the sea toward Capernaum. And it was already dark, and Jesus had not come to them. [18] Then the sea arose because a great wind was blowing. [19] So when they had rowed about three or four miles, they saw Jesus walking on the sea and drawing near the boat; and they were afraid. [20] But He said to them, "It is I; do not be afraid." [21] Then they willingly received Him into the boat, and immediately the boat was at the land where they were going. (NKJV)

12. BLIND BARTIMAEUS RECEIVES SIGHT

Matthew 20:29-34

Mark 10:46-52

29 Now as they went out of Jericho, a great multitude followed Him. 30 And behold, two blind men sitting by the road, when they heard that Jesus was passing by, cried out, saying, "Have mercy on us, O Lord, Son of David!"

31 Then the multitude warned them that they should be quiet; but they cried out all the more, saying, "Have mercy on us, O Lord, Son of David!"

32 So Jesus stood still and called them, and said, "What do you want Me to do for you?"

33 They said to Him, "Lord, that our eyes may be opened." 34 So Jesus had compassion and touched their eyes. And immediately their eyes received sight, and they followed Him. (NKJV)

46 Now they came to Jericho. As He went out of Jericho with His disciples and a great multitude, blind Bartimaeus, the son of Timaeus, sat by the road begging. 47 And when he heard that it was Jesus of Nazareth, he began to cry out and say, "Jesus, Son of David, have mercy on me!"

48 Then many warned him to be quiet; but he cried out all the more, "Son of David, have mercy on me!"

49 So Jesus stood still and commanded him to be called.

Then they called the blind man, saying to him, "Be of good cheer. Rise, He is calling you."

50 And throwing aside his garment, he rose and came to Jesus.

51 So Jesus answered and said to him, "What do you want Me to do for you?"

The blind man said to Him, "Rabboni, that I may receive my sight."

52 Then Jesus said to him, "Go your way; your faith has made you well." And immediately he received his sight and followed Jesus on the road. (NKJV)

32

Luke 18:35-43

[35] Then it happened, as He was coming near Jericho, that a certain blind man sat by the road begging. [36] And hearing a multitude passing by, he asked what it meant. [37] So they told him that Jesus of Nazareth was passing by. [38] And he cried out, saying, "Jesus, Son of David, have mercy on me!"

[39] Then those who went before warned him that he should be quiet; but he cried out all the more, "Son of David, have mercy on me!"

[40] So Jesus stood still and commanded him to be brought to Him. And when he had come near, He asked him, [41] saying, "What do you want Me to do for you?"

He said, "Lord, that I may receive my sight."

[42] Then Jesus said to him, "Receive your sight; your faith has made you well." [43] And immediately he received his sight, and followed Him, glorifying God. And all the people, when they saw *it,* gave praise to God. (NKJV)

13. A GIRL IS FREED FROM A DEMON

Matthew 15:21-28

Mark 7:24-30

[21] Then Jesus went out from there and departed to the region of Tyre and Sidon. [22] And behold, a woman of Canaan came from that region and cried out to Him, saying, "Have mercy on me, O Lord, Son of David! My daughter is severely demon-possessed."

[23] But He answered her not a word.

And His disciples came and urged Him, saying, "Send her away, for she cries out after us."

[24] But He answered and said, "I was not sent except to the lost sheep of the house of Israel."

[25] Then she came and worshiped Him, saying, "Lord, help me!"

[26] But He answered and said, "It is not good to take the children's bread and throw it to the little dogs."

[27] And she said, "Yes, Lord, yet even the little dogs eat the crumbs which fall from their masters' table."

[28] Then Jesus answered and said to her, "O woman, great is your faith! Let it be to you as you desire." And her daughter was healed from that very hour. (NKJV)

[24] From there He arose and went to the region of Tyre and Sidon.[h] And He entered a house and wanted no one to know it, but He could not be hidden. [25] For a woman whose young daughter had an unclean spirit heard about Him, and she came and fell at His feet. [26] The woman was a Greek, a Syro-Phoenician by birth, and she kept asking Him to cast the demon out of her daughter. [27] But Jesus said to her, "Let the children be filled first, for it is not good to take the children's bread and throw it to the little dogs."

[28] And she answered and said to Him, "Yes, Lord, yet even the little dogs under the table eat from the children's crumbs."

[29] Then He said to her, "For this saying go your way; the demon has gone out of your daughter."

[30] And when she had come to her house, she found the demon gone out, and her daughter lying on the bed. (NKJV)

14. FOUR THOUSAND ARE FED

Matthew 15:32-38

Mark 8:1-9

³² Now Jesus called His disciples to *Himself* and said, "I have compassion on the multitude, because they have now continued with Me three days and have nothing to eat. And I do not want to send them away hungry, lest they faint on the way."

³³ Then His disciples said to Him, "Where could we get enough bread in the wilderness to fill such a great multitude?"

³⁴ Jesus said to them, "How many loaves do you have?"

And they said, "Seven, and a few little fish."

³⁵ So He commanded the multitude to sit down on the ground. ³⁶ And He took the seven loaves and the fish and gave thanks, broke *them* and gave *them* to His disciples; and the disciples *gave* to the multitude. ³⁷ So they all ate and were filled, and they took up seven large baskets full of the fragments that were left. ³⁸ Now those who ate were four thousand men, besides women and children. (NKJV)

¹ In those days, the multitude being very great and having nothing to eat, Jesus called His disciples *to Him* and said to them, ² "I have compassion on the multitude, because they have now continued with Me three days and have nothing to eat. ³ And if I send them away hungry to their own houses, they will faint on the way; for some of them have come from afar."

⁴ Then His disciples answered Him, "How can one satisfy these people with bread here in the wilderness?"

⁵ He asked them, "How many loaves do you have?"

And they said, "Seven."

⁶ So He commanded the multitude to sit down on the ground. And He took the seven loaves and gave thanks, broke *them* and gave *them* to His disciples to set before *them;* and they set *them* before the multitude. ⁷ They also had a few small fish; and having blessed them, He said to set them also before *them.* ⁸ So they ate and were filled, and they took up seven large baskets of leftover fragments. (NKJV)

15. CURSING THE FIG TREE

Matthew 21:18-22

[18] Now in the morning, as He returned to the city, He was hungry. [19] And seeing a fig tree by the road, He came to it and found nothing on it but leaves, and said to it, "Let no fruit grow on you ever again." Immediately the fig tree withered away.

[20] And when the disciples saw *it,* they marveled, saying, "How did the fig tree wither away so soon?"

[21] So Jesus answered and said to them, "Assuredly, I say to you, if you have faith and do not doubt, you will not only do what was done to the fig tree, but also if you say to this mountain, 'Be removed and be cast into the sea,' it will be done. [22] And whatever things you ask in prayer, believing, you will receive." (NKJV)

Mark 11:12-14, 20-24

[12] Now the next day, when they had come out from Bethany, He was hungry. [13] And seeing from afar a fig tree having leaves, He went to see if perhaps He would find something on it. When He came to it, He found nothing but leaves, for it was not the season for figs. [14] In response Jesus said to it, "Let no one eat fruit from you ever again."

And His disciples heard *it.*

[20] Now in the morning, as they passed by, they saw the fig tree dried up from the roots. [21] And Peter, remembering, said to Him, "Rabbi, look! The fig tree which You cursed has withered away."

[22] So Jesus answered and said to them, "Have faith in God. [23] For assuredly, I say to you, whoever says to this mountain, 'Be removed and be cast into the sea,' and does not doubt in his heart, but believes that those things he says will be done, he will have whatever he says. [24] Therefore I say to you, whatever things you ask when you pray, believe that you receive *them,* and you will have *them.* (NKJV)

"Lion of Judah" By Barry L. Barnes

16. A CENTURION'S SERVANT IS HEALED

Matthew 8:5-13

[5] Now when Jesus had entered Capernaum, a centurion came to Him, pleading with Him, [6] saying, "Lord, my servant is lying at home paralyzed, dreadfully tormented."

[7] And Jesus said to him, "I will come and heal him."

[8] The centurion answered and said, "Lord, I am not worthy that You should come under my roof. But only speak a word, and my servant will be healed. [9] For I also am a man under authority, having soldiers under me. And I say to this *one,* 'Go,' and he goes; and to another, 'Come,' and he comes; and to my servant, 'Do this,' and he does *it.*"

[10] When Jesus heard *it,* He marveled, and said to those who followed, "Assuredly, I say to you, I have not found such great faith, not even in Israel! [11] And I say to you that many will come from east and west, and sit down with Abraham, Isaac, and Jacob in the kingdom of heaven. [12] But the sons of the kingdom will be cast out into outer darkness. There will be weeping and gnashing of teeth." [13] Then Jesus said to the centurion, "Go your way; and as you have believed, *so* let it be done for you." And his servant was healed that same hour. (NKJV)

Luke 7:1-10

[1] Now when He concluded all His sayings in the hearing of the people, He entered Capernaum. [2] And a certain centurion's servant, who was dear to him, was sick and ready to die. [3] So when he heard about Jesus, he sent elders of the Jews to Him, pleading with Him to come and heal his servant. [4] And when they came to Jesus, they begged Him earnestly, saying that the one for whom He should do this was deserving, [5] "for he loves our nation, and has built us a synagogue." [6] Then Jesus went with them. And when He was already not far from the house, the centurion sent friends to Him, saying to Him, "Lord, do not trouble Yourself, for I am not worthy that You should enter under my roof. [7] Therefore I did not even think myself worthy to come to You. But say the word, and my servant will be healed. [8] For I also am a man placed under authority, having soldiers under me. And I say to one, 'Go,' and he goes; and to another, 'Come,' and he comes; and to my servant, 'Do this,' and he does *it.*" [9] When Jesus heard these things, He marveled at him, and turned around and said to the crowd that followed Him, "I say to you, I have not found such great faith, not even in Israel!" [10] And those who were sent, returning to the house, found the servant well who had been sick. (NKJV)

17. AN EVIL SPIRIT IS SENT OUT OF A MAN

Mark 1:23-27

[23] Now there was a man in their synagogue with an unclean spirit. And he cried out, [24] saying, "Let *us* alone! What have we to do with You, Jesus of Nazareth? Did You come to destroy us? I know who You are—the Holy One of God!" [25] But Jesus rebuked him, saying, "Be quiet, and come out of him!" [26] And when the unclean spirit had convulsed him and cried out with a loud voice, he came out of him. [27] Then they were all amazed, so that they questioned among themselves, saying, "What is this? What new doctrine *is* this? For with authority He commands even the unclean spirits, and they obey Him." (NKJV)

Luke 4:33-36

[33] Now in the synagogue there was a man who had a spirit of an unclean demon. And he cried out with a loud voice, [34] saying, "Let *us* alone! What have we to do with You, Jesus of Nazareth? Did You come to destroy us? I know who You are—the Holy One of God!" [35] But Jesus rebuked him, saying, "Be quiet, and come out of him!" And when the demon had thrown him in *their* midst, it came out of him and did not hurt him. [36] Then they were all amazed and spoke among themselves, saying, "What a word this *is!* For with authority and power He commands the unclean spirits, and they come out." (NKJV)

18. A MUTE DEMONIAC IS HEALED

Matthew 12:22

²² Then one was brought to Him who was demon-possessed, blind and mute; and He healed him, so that the blind and mute man both spoke and saw. (NKJV)

Luke 11:14

¹⁴ And He was casting out a demon, and it was mute. So it was, when the demon had gone out, that the mute spoke; and the multitudes marveled. (NKJV)

19. TWO BLIND MEN FIND SIGHT

Matthew 9:27-31

²⁷ When Jesus departed from there, two blind men followed Him, crying out and saying, "Son of David, have mercy on us!"
²⁸ And when He had come into the house, the blind men came to Him. And Jesus said to them, "Do you believe that I am able to do this?" They said to Him, "Yes, Lord."
²⁹ Then He touched their eyes, saying, "According to your faith let it be to you." ³⁰ And their eyes were opened. And Jesus sternly warned them, saying, "See *that* no one knows *it.*" ³¹ But when they had departed, they spread the news about Him in all that country. (NKJV)

20. JESUS HEALS THE MUTE MAN

Matthew 9:32, 33

[32] As they went out, behold, they brought to Him a man, mute and demon-possessed. [33] And when the demon was cast out, the mute spoke. And the multitudes marveled, saying, "It was never seen like this in Israel!" (NKJV)

21. A COIN IN A FISH'S MOUTH

Matthew 17:24-27

[24] When they had come to Capernaum, those who received the *temple* tax came to Peter and said, "Does your Teacher not pay the *temple* tax?"

[25] He said, "Yes."

And when he had come into the house, Jesus anticipated him, saying, "What do you think, Simon? From whom do the kings of the earth take customs or taxes, from their sons or from strangers?"

[26] Peter said to Him, "From strangers."

Jesus said to him, "Then the sons are free. [27] Nevertheless, lest we offend them, go to the sea, cast in a hook, and take the fish that comes up first. And when you have opened its mouth, you will find a piece of money; take that and give it to them for Me and you." (NKJV)

22. A DEAF AND MUTE MAN IS HEALED

Mark 7:31-37

[31] Again, departing from the region of Tyre and Sidon, He came through the midst of the region of Decapolis to the Sea of Galilee. [32] Then they brought to Him one who was deaf and had an impediment in his speech, and they begged Him to put His hand on him. [33] And He took him aside from the multitude, and put His fingers in his ears, and He spat and touched his tongue. [34] Then, looking up to heaven, He sighed, and said to him, "Ephphatha," that is, "Be opened."

[35] Immediately his ears were opened, and the impediment of his tongue was loosed, and he spoke plainly. [36] Then He commanded them that they should tell no one; but the more He commanded them, the more widely they proclaimed *it.* [37] And they were astonished beyond measure, saying, "He has done all things well. He makes both the deaf to hear and the mute to speak." (NKJV)

23. A BLIND MAN SEES AT BETHSAIDA

Mark 8:22-26

[22] Then He came to Bethsaida; and they brought a blind man to Him, and begged Him to touch him. [23] So He took the blind man by the hand and led him out of the town. And when He had spit on his eyes and put His hands on him, He asked him if he saw anything.

[24] And he looked up and said, "I see men like trees, walking."

[25] Then He put *His* hands on his eyes again and made him look up. And he was restored and saw everyone clearly. [26] Then He sent him away to his house, saying, "Neither go into the town, nor tell anyone in the town." (NKJV)

24. THE FIRST MIRACULOUS CATCH OF FISH

Luke 5:1-11

[1] So it was, as the multitude pressed about Him to hear the word of God, that He stood by the Lake of Gennesaret, [2] and saw two boats standing by the lake; but the fishermen had gone from them and were washing *their* nets. [3] Then He got into one of the boats, which was Simon's, and asked him to put out a little from the land. And He sat down and taught the multitudes from the boat.

[4] When He had stopped speaking, He said to Simon, "Launch out into the deep and let down your nets for a catch."

[5] But Simon answered and said to Him, "Master, we have toiled all night and caught nothing; nevertheless at Your word I will let down the net." [6] And when they had done this, they caught a great number of fish, and their net was breaking. [7] So they signaled to *their* partners in the other boat to come and help them. And they came and filled both the boats, so that they began to sink. [8] When Simon Peter saw *it,* he fell down at Jesus' knees, saying, "Depart from me, for I am a sinful man, O Lord!"

[9] For he and all who were with him were astonished at the catch of fish which they had taken; [10] and so also *were* James and John, the sons of Zebedee, who were partners with Simon. And Jesus said to Simon, "Do not be afraid. From now on you will catch men." [11] So when they had brought their boats to land, they forsook all and followed Him. (NKJV)

44

25. A WIDOW'S SON IS RAISED

Luke 7:11-16

[11] Now it happened, the day after, *that* He went into a city called Nain; and many of His disciples went with Him, and a large crowd. [12] And when He came near the gate of the city, behold, a dead man was being carried out, the only son of his mother; and she was a widow. And a large crowd from the city was with her. [13] When the Lord saw her, He had compassion on her and said to her, "Do not weep." [14] Then He came and touched the open coffin, and those who carried *him* stood still. And He said, "Young man, I say to you, arise." [15] So he who was dead sat up and began to speak. And He presented him to his mother.

[16] Then fear came upon all, and they glorified God, saying, "A great prophet has risen up among us"; and, "God has visited His people." (NKJV)

26. A CRIPPLED WOMAN IS HEALED

Luke 13:10-17

[10] Now He was teaching in one of the synagogues on the Sabbath. [11] And behold, there was a woman who had a spirit of infirmity eighteen years, and was bent over and could in no way raise *herself* up. [12] But when Jesus saw her, He called *her* to *Him* and said to her, "Woman, you are loosed from your infirmity." [13] And He laid *His* hands on her, and immediately she was made straight, and glorified God.

[14] But the ruler of the synagogue answered with indignation, because Jesus had healed on the Sabbath; and he said to the crowd, "There are six days on which men ought to work; therefore come and be healed on them, and not on the Sabbath day."

[15] The Lord then answered him and said, "Hypocrite! Does not each one of you on the Sabbath loose his ox or donkey from the stall, and lead *it* away to water it? [16] So ought not this woman, being a daughter of Abraham, whom Satan has bound—think of it—for eighteen years, be loosed from this bond on the Sabbath?" [17] And when He said these things, all His adversaries were put to shame; and all the multitude rejoiced for all the glorious things that were done by Him. (NKJV)

46

27. JESUS HEALS A SICK MAN

Luke 14:1-6

[1] Now it happened, as He went into the house of one of the rulers of the Pharisees to eat bread on the Sabbath, that they watched Him closely. [2] And behold, there was a certain man before Him who had dropsy. [3] And Jesus, answering, spoke to the lawyers and Pharisees, saying, "Is it lawful to heal on the Sabbath?"
[4] But they kept silent. And He took *him* and healed him, and let him go. [5] Then He answered them, saying, "Which of you, having a donkey or an ox that has fallen into a pit, will not immediately pull him out on the Sabbath day?" [6] And they could not answer Him regarding these things. (NKJV)

28. TEN LEPERS ARE HEALED

Luke 17:11-19

[11] Now it happened as He went to Jerusalem that He passed through the midst of Samaria and Galilee. [12] Then as He entered a certain village, there met Him ten men who were lepers, who stood afar off. [13] And they lifted up *their* voices and said, "Jesus, Master, have mercy on us!"
[14] So when He saw *them,* He said to them, "Go, show yourselves to the priests." And so it was that as they went, they were cleansed.
[15] And one of them, when he saw that he was healed, returned, and with a loud voice glorified God, [16] and fell down on *his* face at His feet, giving Him thanks. And he was a Samaritan.
[17] So Jesus answered and said, "Were there not ten cleansed? But where *are* the nine? [18] Were there not any found who returned to give glory to God except this foreigner?" [19] And He said to him, "Arise, go your way. Your faith has made you well." (NKJV)

29. JESUS RESTORES A MAN'S EAR

Luke 22:47-51

[47] And while He was still speaking, behold, a multitude; and he who was called Judas, one of the twelve, went before them and drew near to Jesus to kiss Him. [48] But Jesus said to him, "Judas, are you betraying the Son of Man with a kiss?"
[49] When those around Him saw what was going to happen, they said to Him, "Lord, shall we strike with the sword?" [50] And one of them struck the servant of the high priest and cut off his right ear.
[51] But Jesus answered and said, "Permit even this." And He touched his ear and healed him. (NKJV)

30. JESUS TURNS WATER INTO WINE

John 2:1-11

[1] On the third day there was a wedding in Cana of Galilee, and the mother of Jesus was there. [2] Now both Jesus and His disciples were invited to the wedding. [3] And when they ran out of wine, the mother of Jesus said to Him, "They have no wine."
[4] Jesus said to her, "Woman, what does your concern have to do with Me? My hour has not yet come."
[5] His mother said to the servants, "Whatever He says to you, do *it*."
[6] Now there were set there six waterpots of stone, according to the manner of purification of the Jews, containing twenty or thirty gallons apiece. [7] Jesus said to them, "Fill the waterpots with water." And they filled them up to the brim. [8] And He said to them, "Draw *some* out now, and take *it* to the master of the feast." And they took *it*. [9] When the master of the feast had tasted the water that was made wine, and did not know where it came from (but the servants who had drawn the water knew), the master of the feast called the bridegroom. [10] And he said to him,

"Every man at the beginning sets out the good wine, and when the *guests* have well drunk, then the inferior. You have kept the good wine until now!"

[11] This beginning of signs Jesus did in Cana of Galilee, and manifested His glory; and His disciples believed in Him. (NKJV)

31. AN OFFICIAL'S SON IS HEALED AT CANA

John 4:46-54

[46] So Jesus came again to Cana of Galilee where He had made the water wine. And there was a certain nobleman whose son was sick at Capernaum. [47] When he heard that Jesus had come out of Judea into Galilee, he went to Him and implored Him to come down and heal his son, for he was at the point of death. [48] Then Jesus said to him, "Unless you *people* see signs and wonders, you will by no means believe."

[49] The nobleman said to Him, "Sir, come down before my child dies!"

[50] Jesus said to him, "Go your way; your son lives." So the man believed the word that Jesus spoke to him, and he went his way. [51] And as he was now going down, his servants met him and told *him,* saying, "Your son lives!"

[52] Then he inquired of them the hour when he got better. And they said to him, "Yesterday at the seventh hour the fever left him." [53] So the father knew that *it was* at the same hour in which Jesus said to him, "Your son lives." And he himself believed, and his whole household.

[54] This again *is* the second sign Jesus did when He had come out of Judea into Galilee. (NKJV)

32. A LAME MAN IS HEALED

John 5:1-16

¹ After this there was a feast of the Jews, and Jesus went up to Jerusalem. ² Now there is in Jerusalem by the Sheep *Gate* a pool, which is called in Hebrew, Bethesda, having five porches. ³ In these lay a great multitude of sick people, blind, lame, paralyzed, waiting for the moving of the water. ⁴ For an angel went down at a certain time into the pool and stirred up the water; then whoever stepped in first, after the stirring of the water, was made well of whatever disease he had. ⁵ Now a certain man was there who had an infirmity thirty-eight years. ⁶ When Jesus saw him lying there, and knew that he already had been *in that condition* a long time, He said to him, "Do you want to be made well?" ⁷ The sick man answered Him, "Sir, I have no man to put me into the pool when the water is stirred up; but while I am coming, another steps down before me." ⁸ Jesus said to him, "Rise, take up your bed and walk." ⁹ And immediately the man was made well, took up his bed, and walked.

And that day was the Sabbath. ¹⁰ The Jews therefore said to him who was cured, "It is the Sabbath; it is not lawful for you to carry your bed." ¹¹ He answered them, "He who made me well said to me, 'Take up your bed and walk.'" ¹² Then they asked him, "Who is the Man who said to you, 'Take up your bed and walk'?" ¹³ But the one who was healed did not know who it was, for Jesus had withdrawn, a multitude being in *that* place. ¹⁴ Afterward Jesus found him in the temple, and said to him, "See, you have been made well. Sin no more, lest a worse thing come upon you." ¹⁵ The man departed and told the Jews that it was Jesus who had made him well. ¹⁶ For this reason the Jews persecuted Jesus, and sought to kill Him, because He had done these things on the Sabbath. (NKJV)

33. JESUS HEALS A MAN BORN BLIND

John 9:1-7

[1] Now as *Jesus* passed by, He saw a man who was blind from birth. [2] And His disciples asked Him, saying, "Rabbi, who sinned, this man or his parents, that he was born blind?"

[3] Jesus answered, "Neither this man nor his parents sinned, but that the works of God should be revealed in him. [4] I must work the works of Him who sent Me while it is day; *the* night is coming when no one can work. [5] As long as I am in the world, I am the light of the world."

[6] When He had said these things, He spat on the ground and made clay with the saliva; and He anointed the eyes of the blind man with the clay.

[7] And He said to him, "Go, wash in the pool of Siloam" (which is translated, Sent). So he went and washed, and came back seeing. (NKJV)

"New Day" By Barry L. Barnes

34. LAZARUS IS RAISED FROM THE DEAD

John 11:1-45

Now a certain man was ill, Lazarus of Bethany, the village of Mary and her sister Martha. [2]Mary was the one who anointed the Lord with perfume and wiped his feet with her hair; her brother Lazarus was ill. [3]So the sisters sent a message to Jesus, 'Lord, he whom you love is ill.' [4]But when Jesus heard it, he said, 'This illness does not lead to death; rather it is for God's glory, so that the Son of God may be glorified through it.' [5]Accordingly, though Jesus loved Martha and her sister and Lazarus, [6]after having heard that Lazarus was ill, he stayed two days longer in the place where he was.

7 Then after this he said to the disciples, 'Let us go to Judea again.' [8]The disciples said to him, 'Rabbi, the Jews were just now trying to stone you, and are you going there again?' [9]Jesus answered, 'Are there not twelve hours of daylight? Those who walk during the day do not stumble, because they see the light of this world. [10]But those who walk at night stumble, because the light is not in them.' [11]After saying this, he told them, 'Our friend Lazarus has fallen asleep, but I am going there to awaken him.' [12]The disciples said to him, 'Lord, if he has fallen asleep, he will be all right.' [13]Jesus, however, had been speaking about his death, but they thought that he was referring merely to sleep. [14]Then Jesus told them plainly, 'Lazarus is dead. [15]For your sake I am glad I was not there, so that you may believe. But let us go to him.' [16]Thomas, who was called the Twin,* said to his fellow-disciples, 'Let us also go, that we may die with him.'

17 When Jesus arrived, he found that Lazarus* had already been in the tomb for four days. [18]Now Bethany was near Jerusalem, some two miles away, [19]and many of the Jews had come to Martha and Mary to console them about their brother. [20]When Martha heard that Jesus was coming, she went and met him, while Mary stayed at home. [21]Martha said to Jesus, 'Lord, if you had been here, my brother would not have died. [22]But even now I know that God will give you whatever you ask of him.' [23]Jesus said to her, 'Your brother will rise again.' [24]Martha said to him, 'I know that he will rise again in the resurrection on the last day.' [25]Jesus said to her,

'I am the resurrection and the life.- Those who believe in me, even though they die, will live, [26]and everyone who lives and believes in me will never die. Do you believe this?' [27]She said to him, 'Yes, Lord, I believe that you are the Messiah, the Son of God, the one coming into the world.'

28 When she had said this, she went back and called her sister Mary, and told her privately, 'The Teacher is here and is calling for you.' [29]And when she heard it, she got up quickly and went to him. [30]Now Jesus had not yet come to the village, but was still at the place where Martha had met him. [31]The Jews who were with her in the house, consoling her, saw Mary get up quickly and go out. They followed her because they thought that she was going to the tomb to weep there. [32]When Mary came where Jesus was and saw him, she knelt at his feet and said to him, 'Lord, if you had been here, my brother would not have died.' [33]When Jesus saw her weeping, and the Jews who came with her also weeping, he was greatly disturbed in spirit and deeply moved. [34]He said, 'Where have you laid him?' They said to him, 'Lord, come and see.'

[35]Jesus began to weep. [36]So the Jews said, 'See how he loved him!' [37]But some of them said, 'Could not he who opened the eyes of the blind man have kept this man from dying?'

38 Then Jesus, again greatly disturbed, came to the tomb. It was a cave, and a stone was lying against it. [39]Jesus said, 'Take away the stone.' Martha, the sister of the dead man, said to him, 'Lord, already there is a stench because he has been dead for four days.' [40]Jesus said to her, 'Did I not tell you that if you believed, you would see the glory of God?' [41]So they took away the stone. And Jesus looked upwards and said, 'Father, I thank you for having heard me. [42]I knew that you always hear me, but I have said this for the sake of the crowd standing here, so that they may believe that you sent me.' [43]When he had said this, he cried with a loud voice, 'Lazarus, come out!' [44]The dead man came out, his hands and feet bound with strips of cloth, and his face wrapped in a cloth. Jesus said to them, 'Unbind him, and let him go.'

45 Many of the Jews therefore, who had come with Mary and had seen what Jesus did, believed in him. (NRSV)

35. THE SECOND MIRACULOUS CATCH OF FISH

John 21:1-14

21After these things Jesus showed himself again to the disciples by the Sea of Tiberias; and he showed himself in this way. [2]Gathered there together were Simon Peter, Thomas called the Twin, Nathanael of Cana in Galilee, the sons of Zebedee, and two others of his disciples. [3]Simon Peter said to them, 'I am going fishing.' They said to him, 'We will go with you.' They went out and got into the boat, but that night they caught nothing.

4 Just after daybreak, Jesus stood on the beach; but the disciples did not know that it was Jesus. [5]Jesus said to them, 'Children, you have no fish, have you?' They answered him, 'No.' [6]He said to them, 'Cast the net to the right side of the boat, and you will find some.' So they cast it, and now they were not able to haul it in because there were so many fish. [7]That disciple whom Jesus loved said to Peter, 'It is the Lord!' When Simon Peter heard that it was the Lord, he put on some clothes, for he was naked, and jumped into the lake. [8]But the other disciples came in the boat, dragging the net full of fish, for they were not far from the land, only about a hundred yards off.

9 When they had gone ashore, they saw a charcoal fire there, with fish on it, and bread. [10]Jesus said to them, 'Bring some of the fish that you have just caught.' [11]So Simon Peter went aboard and hauled the net ashore, full of large fish, a hundred and fifty-three of them; and though there were so many, the net was not torn. [12]Jesus said to them, 'Come and have breakfast.' Now none of the disciples dared to ask him, 'Who are you?' because they knew it was the Lord. [13]Jesus came and took the bread and gave it to them, and did the same with the fish. [14]This was now the third time that Jesus appeared to the disciples after he was raised from the dead. (NRSV)

"Heavenly Sonset" By Barry L. Barnes

Part II: The Parables of Jesus

TEACHING PARABLES ABOUT THE KINGDOM OF GOD

1. The Soils

Matthew 13:3-8

[3]And he told them many things in parables, saying: 'Listen! A sower went out to sow. [4]And as he sowed, some seeds fell on the path, and the birds came and ate them up. [5]Other seeds fell on rocky ground, where they did not have much soil, and they sprang up quickly, since they had no depth of soil. [6]But when the sun rose, they were scorched; and since they had no root, they withered away. [7]Other seeds fell among thorns, and the thorns grew up and choked them. [8]Other seeds fell on good soil and brought forth grain, some a hundredfold, some sixty, some thirty. (NRSV)

Mark 4:4-8

[4]And as he sowed, some seed fell on the path, and the birds came and ate it up. [5]Other seed fell on rocky ground, where it did not have much soil, and it sprang up quickly, since it had no depth of soil. [6]And when the sun rose, it was scorched; and since it had no root, it withered away. [7]Other seed fell among thorns, and the thorns grew up and choked it, and it yielded no grain. [8]Other seed fell into good soil and brought forth grain, growing up and increasing and yielding thirty and sixty and a hundredfold.' (NRSV)

Luke 8:5-8

[5]'A sower went out to sow his seed; and as he sowed, some fell on the path and was trampled on, and the birds of the air ate it up. [6]Some fell on the rock; and as it grew up, it withered for lack of moisture. [7]Some fell among thorns, and the thorns grew with it and choked it. [8]Some fell into good soil, and when it grew, it produced a hundredfold.' As he said this, he called out, 'Let anyone with ears to hear listen!' (NRSV)

2. The Weeds

Matthew 13:24-30

24 He put before them another parable: 'The kingdom of heaven may be compared to someone who sowed good seed in his field; [25]but while everybody was asleep, an enemy came and sowed weeds among the wheat, and then went away. [26]So when the plants came up and bore grain, then the weeds appeared as well. [27]And the slaves of the householder came and said to him, "Master, did you not sow good seed in your field? Where, then, did these weeds come from?" [28]He answered, "An enemy has done this." The slaves said to him, "Then do you want us to go and gather them?" [29]But he replied, "No; for in gathering the weeds you would uproot the wheat along with them. [30]Let both of them grow together until the harvest; and at harvest time I will tell the reapers, Collect the weeds first and bind them in bundles to be burned, but gather the wheat into my barn." '
(NRSV)

3. The Mustard Seed

Matthew 13:31, 32

31 He put before them another parable: 'The kingdom of heaven is like a mustard seed that someone took and sowed in his field; ^{32}it is the smallest of all the seeds, but when it has grown it is the greatest of shrubs and becomes a tree, so that the birds of the air come and make nests in its branches.' (NRSV)

Mark 4:30-32

30 He also said, 'With what can we compare the kingdom of God, or what parable will we use for it? ^{31}It is like a mustard seed, which, when sown upon the ground, is the smallest of all the seeds on earth; ^{32}yet when it is sown it grows up and becomes the greatest of all shrubs, and puts forth large branches, so that the birds of the air can make nests in its shade.' (NRSV)

18 He said therefore, 'What is the kingdom of God like? And to what should I compare it? [19]It is like a mustard seed that someone took and sowed in the garden; it grew and became a tree, and the birds of the air made nests in its branches.'(NRSV)

"The Garden" By Barry L. Barnes

4. The Yeast

Matthew 13:33

33 He told them another parable: 'The kingdom of heaven is like yeast that a woman took and mixed in with three measures of flour until all of it was leavened.' (NRSV)

Luke 13:20, 21

20 And again he said, 'To what should I compare the kingdom of God? [21]It is like yeast that a woman took and mixed in with three measures of flour until all of it was leavened.' (NRSV)

5. The Treasure

Matthew 13:44

44 'The kingdom of heaven is like treasure hidden in a field, which someone found and hid; then in his joy he goes and sells all that he has and buys that field. (NRSV)

6. The Pearl

Matthew 13:45, 46

45 'Again, the kingdom of heaven is like a merchant in search of fine pearls; [46]on finding one pearl of great value, he went and sold all that he had and bought it. (NRSV)

7. The Fishing Net

Matthew 13:47-50

47 'Again, the kingdom of heaven is like a net that was thrown into the sea and caught fish of every kind; [48]when it was full, they drew it ashore, sat down, and put the good into baskets but threw out the bad. [49]So it will be at the end of the age. The angels will come out and separate the evil from the righteous [50]and throw them into the furnace of fire, where there will be weeping and gnashing of teeth. (NRSV)

8. The Growing Wheat

Mark 4:26-29

26 He also said, 'The kingdom of God is as if someone would scatter seed on the ground, [27]and would sleep and rise night and day, and the seed would sprout and grow, he does not know how. [28]The earth produces of itself, first the stalk, then the head, then the full grain in the head. [29]But when the grain is ripe, at once he goes in with his sickle, because the harvest has come.' (NRSV)

TEACHING PARABLES
ABOUT SERVICE AND OBEDIENCE

9. The Workers in the Harvest

Matthew 20:1-16

'For the kingdom of heaven is like a landowner who went out early in the morning to hire labourers for his vineyard. [2]After agreeing with the labourers for the usual daily wage, he sent them into his vineyard. [3]When he went out about nine o'clock, he saw others standing idle in the market-place; [4]and he said to them, "You also go into the vineyard, and I will pay you whatever is right." So they went. [5]When he went out again about noon and about three o'clock, he did the same. [6]And about five o'clock he went out and found others standing around; and he said to them, "Why are you standing here idle all day?" [7]They said to him, "Because no one has hired us." He said to them, "You also go into the vineyard." [8]When evening came, the owner of the vineyard said to his manager, "Call the labourers and give them their pay, beginning with the last and then going to the first." [9]When those hired about five o'clock came, each of them received the usual daily wage. [10]Now when the first came, they thought they would receive more; but each of them also received the usual daily wage. [11]And when they received it, they grumbled against the landowner, [12]saying, "These last worked only one hour, and you have made them equal to us who have borne the burden of the day and the scorching heat." [13]But he replied to one of them, "Friend, I am doing you no wrong; did you not agree with me for the usual daily wage? [14]Take what belongs to you and go; I choose to give to this last the same as I give to you. [15]Am I not allowed to do what I choose with what belongs to me? Or are you envious because I am generous?" [16]So the last will be first, and the first will be last.' (NRSV)

10. The Loaned Money

Matthew 25:14-30

14 'For it is as if a man, going on a journey, summoned his slaves and entrusted his property to them; [15]to one he gave five talents, to another two, to another one, to each according to his ability. Then he went away. [16]The one who had received the five talents went off at once and traded with them, and made five more talents. [17]In the same way, the one who had the two talents made two more talents. [18]But the one who had received the one talent went off and dug a hole in the ground and hid his master's money. [19]After a long time the master of those slaves came and settled accounts with them. [20]Then the one who had received the five talents came forward, bringing five more talents, saying, "Master, you handed over to me five talents; see, I have made five more talents." [21]His master said to him, "Well done, good and trustworthy slave; you have been trustworthy in a few things, I will put you in charge of many things; enter into the joy of your master." [22]And the one with the two talents also came forward, saying, "Master, you handed over to me two talents; see, I have made two more talents." [23]His master said to him, "Well done, good and trustworthy slave; you have been trustworthy in a few things, I will put you in charge of many things; enter into the joy of your master." [24]Then the one who had received the one talent also came forward, saying, "Master, I knew that you were a harsh man, reaping where you did not sow, and gathering where you did not scatter seed; [25]so I was afraid, and I went and hid your talent in the ground. Here you have what is yours." [26]But his master replied, "You wicked and lazy slave! You knew, did you, that I reap where I did not sow, and gather where I did not scatter? [27]Then you ought to have invested my money with the bankers, and on my return I would have received what was my own with interest. [28]So take the talent from him, and give it to the one with the ten talents. [29]For to all those who have, more will be given, and they will have an abundance; but from those who have nothing, even what they have will be taken away. [30]As for this worthless slave, throw him into the outer darkness, where there will be weeping and gnashing of teeth." (NRSV)

11. The Nobleman's Servants

Luke 19:11-27

11 As they were listening to this, he went on to tell a parable, because he was near Jerusalem, and because they supposed that the kingdom of God was to appear immediately. ^{12}So he said, 'A nobleman went to a distant country to get royal power for himself and then return. ^{13}He summoned ten of his slaves, and gave them ten pounds, and said to them, "Do business with these until I come back." ^{14}But the citizens of his country hated him and sent a delegation after him, saying, "We do not want this man to rule over us." ^{15}When he returned, having received royal power, he ordered these slaves, to whom he had given the money, to be summoned so that he might find out what they had gained by trading. ^{16}The first came forward and said, "Lord, your pound has made ten more pounds." ^{17}He said to him, "Well done, good slave! Because you have been trustworthy in a very small thing, take charge of ten cities." ^{18}Then the second came, saying, "Lord, your pound has made five pounds." ^{19}He said to him, "And you, rule over five cities." ^{20}Then the other came, saying, "Lord, here is your pound. I wrapped it up in a piece of cloth, ^{21}for I was afraid of you, because you are a harsh man; you take what you did not deposit, and reap what you did not sow." ^{22}He said to him, "I will judge you by your own words, you wicked slave! You knew, did you, that I was a harsh man, taking what I did not deposit and reaping what I did not sow? ^{23}Why then did you not put my money into the bank? Then when I returned, I could have collected it with interest." ^{24}He said to the bystanders, "Take the pound from him and give it to the one who has ten pounds." ^{25}(And they said to him, "Lord, he has ten pounds!") ^{26}"I tell you, to all those who have, more will be given; but from those who have nothing, even what they have will be taken away. ^{27}But as for these enemies of mine who did not want me to be king over them—bring them here and slaughter them in my presence." ' (NRSV)

12. The Servant's Role

Luke 17:7-10

7 'Who among you would say to your slave who has just come in from ploughing or tending sheep in the field, "Come here at once and take your place at the table"? [8]Would you not rather say to him, "Prepare supper for me, put on your apron and serve me while I eat and drink; later you may eat and drink"? [9]Do you thank the slave for doing what was commanded? [10]So you also, when you have done all that you were ordered to do, say, "We are worthless slaves; we have done only what we ought to have done!" ' (NRSV)

TEACHING PARABLES ABOUT PRAYER

13. The Friend At Midnight

Luke 11:5-8

5 And he said to them, 'Suppose one of you has a friend, and you go to him at midnight and say to him, "Friend, lend me three loaves of bread; [6]for a friend of mine has arrived, and I have nothing to set before him." [7]And he answers from within, "Do not bother me; the door has already been locked, and my children are with me in bed; I cannot get up and give you anything." [8]I tell you, even though he will not get up and give him anything because he is his friend, at least because of his persistence he will get up and give him whatever he needs. (NRSV)

14. The Unjust Judge

Luke 18:1-8

Then Jesus told them a parable about their need to pray always and not to lose heart. [2]He said, 'In a certain city there was a judge who neither feared God nor had respect for people. [3]In that city there was a widow who kept coming to him and saying, "Grant me justice against my opponent." [4]For a while he refused; but later he said to himself, "Though I have no fear of God and no respect for anyone, [5]yet because this widow keeps bothering me, I will grant her justice, so that she may not wear me out by continually coming." ' [6]And the Lord said, 'Listen to what the unjust judge says. [7]And will not God grant justice to his chosen ones who cry to him day and night? Will he delay long in helping them? [8]I tell you, he will quickly grant justice to them. And yet, when the Son of Man comes, will he find faith on earth?' (NRSV)

TEACHING PARABLES
ABOUT NEIGHBORS

15. The Good Samaritan
Luke 10:30-37

[30]Jesus replied, 'A man was going down from Jerusalem to Jericho, and fell into the hands of robbers, who stripped him, beat him, and went away, leaving him half dead. [31]Now by chance a priest was going down that road; and when he saw him, he passed by on the other side. [32]So likewise a Levite, when he came to the place and saw him, passed by on the other side. [33]But a Samaritan while travelling came near him; and when he saw him, he was moved with pity. [34]He went to him and bandaged his wounds, having poured oil and wine on them. Then he put him on his own animal, brought him to an inn, and took care of him. [35]The next day he took out two denarii, gave them to the innkeeper, and said, "Take care of him; and when I come back, I will repay you whatever more you spend." [36]Which of these three, do you think, was a neighbour to the man who fell into the hands of the robbers?' [37]He said, 'The one who showed him mercy.' Jesus said to him, 'Go and do likewise.' (NRSV)

TEACHING PARABLES ABOUT HUMILITY

16. The Wedding Feast

Luke 14:7-11

7 When he noticed how the guests chose the places of honour, he told them a parable. [8]'When you are invited by someone to a wedding banquet, do not sit down at the place of honour, in case someone more distinguished than you has been invited by your host; [9]and the host who invited both of you may come and say to you, "Give this person your place", and then in disgrace you would start to take the lowest place. [10]But when you are invited, go and sit down at the lowest place, so that when your host comes, he may say to you, "Friend, move up higher"; then you will be honoured in the presence of all who sit at the table with you. [11]For all who exalt themselves will be humbled, and those who humble themselves will be exalted.' (NRSV)

17. The Proud Pharisee and the Corrupt Tax Collector

Luke 18:9-14

9 He also told this parable to some who trusted in themselves that they were righteous and regarded others with contempt: [10]'Two men went up to the temple to pray, one a Pharisee and the other a tax-collector. [11]The Pharisee, standing by himself, was praying thus, "God, I thank you that I am not like other people: thieves, rogues, adulterers, or even like this tax-collector. [12]I fast twice a week; I give a tenth of all my income." [13]But the tax-collector, standing far off, would not even look up to heaven, but was beating his breast and saying, "God, be merciful to me, a sinner!" [14]I tell you, this man went down to his home justified rather than the other; for all who exalt themselves will be humbled, but all who humble themselves will be exalted.' (NRSV)

TEACHING PARABLES
ABOUT WEALTH

18. The Rich Fool
Luke 12:16-21

[16]Then he told them a parable: 'The land of a rich man produced abundantly. [17]And he thought to himself, "What should I do, for I have no place to store my crops?" [18]Then he said, "I will do this: I will pull down my barns and build larger ones, and there I will store all my grain and my goods. [19]And I will say to my soul, Soul, you have ample goods laid up for many years; relax, eat, drink, be merry." [20]But God said to him, "You fool! This very night your life is being demanded of you. And the things you have prepared, whose will they be?" [21]So it is with those who store up treasures for themselves but are not rich towards God.' (NRSV)

19. The Great Feast
Luke 14:16-24

[16]Then Jesus said to him, 'Someone gave a great dinner and invited many. [17]At the time for the dinner he sent his slave to say to those who had been invited, "Come; for everything is ready now." [18]But they all alike began to make excuses. The first said to him, "I have bought a piece of land, and I must go out and see it; please accept my apologies." [19]Another said, "I have bought five yoke of oxen, and I am going to try them out; please accept my apologies." [20]Another said, "I have just been married, and therefore I cannot come." [21]So the slave returned and reported this to his master. Then the owner of the house became angry and said to his slave, "Go out at once into the streets and lanes of the town and bring in the poor, the crippled, the blind, and the lame." [22]And the slave said, "Sir, what you ordered has been done, and there is still room." [23]Then the master said to the slave, "Go out into the roads and

lanes, and compel people to come in, so that my house may be filled. [24]For I tell you, none of those who were invited will taste my dinner." '
(NRSV)

20. The Shrewd Manager

Luke 16:1-9

Then Jesus said to the disciples, 'There was a rich man who had a manager, and charges were brought to him that this man was squandering his property. [2]So he summoned him and said to him, "What is this that I hear about you? Give me an account of your management, because you cannot be my manager any longer." [3]Then the manager said to himself, "What will I do, now that my master is taking the position away from me? I am not strong enough to dig, and I am ashamed to beg. [4]I have decided what to do so that, when I am dismissed as manager, people may welcome me into their homes." [5]So, summoning his master's debtors one by one, he asked the first, "How much do you owe my master?" [6]He answered, "A hundred jugs of olive oil." He said to him, "Take your bill, sit down quickly, and make it fifty." [7]Then he asked another, "And how much do you owe?" He replied, "A hundred containers of wheat." He said to him, "Take your bill and make it eighty." [8]And his master commended the dishonest manager because he had acted shrewdly; for the children of this age are more shrewd in dealing with their own generation than are the children of light. [9]And I tell you, make friends for yourselves by means of dishonest wealth so that when it is gone, they may welcome you into the eternal homes. (NRSV)

GOSPEL PARABLES
ABOUT GOD'S LOVE

21. The Lost Sheep
Matthew 18:12-14

[12]What do you think? If a shepherd has a hundred sheep, and one of them has gone astray, does he not leave the ninety-nine on the mountains and go in search of the one that went astray? [13]And if he finds it, truly I tell you, he rejoices over it more than over the ninety-nine that never went astray. [14]So it is not the will of your* Father in heaven that one of these little ones should be lost. (NRSV)

Luke 15:3-7

3 So he told them this parable: [4]"Which one of you, having a hundred sheep and losing one of them, does not leave the ninety-nine in the wilderness and go after the one that is lost until he finds it? [5]When he has found it, he lays it on his shoulders and rejoices. [6]And when he comes home, he calls together his friends and neighbours, saying to them, "Rejoice with me, for I have found my sheep that was lost." [7]Just so, I tell you, there will be more joy in heaven over one sinner who repents than over ninety-nine righteous people who need no repentance. (NRSV)

22. The Lost Coin

Luke 15:8-10

8 'Or what woman having ten silver coins, if she loses one of them, does not light a lamp, sweep the house, and search carefully until she finds it? [9]When she has found it, she calls together her friends and neighbours, saying, "Rejoice with me, for I have found the coin that I had lost." [10]Just so, I tell you, there is joy in the presence of the angels of God over one sinner who repents.' (NRSV)

23. The Lost Son

Luke 15:11-32

11 Then Jesus said, 'There was a man who had two sons. [12]The younger of them said to his father, "Father, give me the share of the property that will belong to me." So he divided his property between them. [13]A few days later the younger son gathered all he had and travelled to a distant country, and there he squandered his property in dissolute living. [14]When he had spent everything, a severe famine took place throughout that country, and he began to be in need. [15]So he went and hired himself out to one of the citizens of that country, who sent him to his fields to feed the pigs. [16]He would gladly have filled himself with the pods that the pigs were eating; and no one gave him anything. [17]But when he came to himself he said, "How many of my father's hired hands have bread enough and to spare, but here I am dying of hunger! [18]I will get up and go to my father, and I will say to him, 'Father, I have sinned against heaven and before you; [19]I am no longer worthy to be called your son; treat me like one of your hired hands.' " [20]So he set off and went to his

father. But while he was still far off, his father saw him and was filled with compassion; he ran and put his arms around him and kissed him. [21]Then the son said to him, "Father, I have sinned against heaven and before you; I am no longer worthy to be called your son." [22]But the father said to his slaves, "Quickly, bring out a robe—the best one—and put it on him; put a ring on his finger and sandals on his feet. [23]And get the fatted calf and kill it, and let us eat and celebrate; [24]for this son of mine was dead and is alive again; he was lost and is found!" And they began to celebrate.

25 'Now his elder son was in the field; and when he came and approached the house, he heard music and dancing. [26]He called one of the slaves and asked what was going on. [27]He replied, "Your brother has come, and your father has killed the fatted calf, because he has got him back safe and sound." [28]Then he became angry and refused to go in. His father came out and began to plead with him. [29]But he answered his father, "Listen! For all these years I have been working like a slave for you, and I have never disobeyed your command; yet you have never given me even a young goat so that I might celebrate with my friends. [30]But when this son of yours came back, who has devoured your property with prostitutes, you killed the fatted calf for him!" [31]Then the father said to him, "Son, you are always with me, and all that is mine is yours. [32]But we had to celebrate and rejoice, because this brother of yours was dead and has come to life; he was lost and has been found." (NRSV)

GOSPEL PARABLES
ABOUT THANKFULNESS

24. The Forgiven Debts
Luke 7:41-43

[41]'A certain creditor had two debtors; one owed five hundred denarii, and the other fifty. [42]When they could not pay, he cancelled the debts for both of them. Now which of them will love him more?' [43]Simon answered, 'I suppose the one for whom he cancelled the greater debt.' And Jesus said to him, 'You have judged rightly.' (NRSV)

PARABLES OF JUDGMENT AND
THE FUTURE
ABOUT CHRIST'S RETURN

25. The Ten Virgins
Matthew 25:1-13

'Then the kingdom of heaven will be like this. Ten bridesmaids took their lamps and went to meet the bridegroom. [2]Five of them were foolish, and five were wise. [3]When the foolish took their lamps, they took no oil with them; [4]but the wise took flasks of oil with their lamps. [5]As the bridegroom was delayed, all of them became drowsy and slept. [6]But at midnight there was a shout, "Look! Here is the bridegroom! Come out to meet him." [7]Then all those bridesmaids got up and trimmed their lamps. [8]The foolish said to the wise, "Give us some of your oil, for our lamps are going out." [9]But the wise replied, "No! there will not be enough for you and for us; you had better go to the dealers and buy some for yourselves." [10]And while they went to buy it, the bridegroom came, and those who were ready went with him into the wedding banquet; and the door was shut. [11]Later the other bridesmaids came also, saying, "Lord, lord, open to us." [12]But he replied, "Truly I tell you, I do not know you." [13]Keep awake therefore, for you know neither the day nor the hour. (NRSV)

"Heavenly Sonrise" By Barry L. Barnes

26. The Wise And The Faithful Servants

Matthew 24:45-51

45 'Who then is the faithful and wise slave, whom his master has put in charge of his household, to give the other slaves their allowance of food at the proper time? ⁴⁶Blessed is that slave whom his master will find at work when he arrives. ⁴⁷Truly I tell you, he will put that one in charge of all his possessions. ⁴⁸But if that wicked slave says to himself, "My master is delayed", ⁴⁹and he begins to beat his fellow-slaves, and eats and drinks with drunkards, ⁵⁰the master of that slave will come on a day when he does not expect him and at an hour that he does not know. ⁵¹He will cut him in pieces and put him with the hypocrites, where there will be weeping and gnashing of teeth. (NRSV)

Luke 12:42-48

⁴²And the Lord said, 'Who then is the faithful and prudent manager whom his master will put in charge of his slaves, to give them their allowance of food at the proper time? ⁴³Blessed is that slave whom his master will find at work when he arrives. ⁴⁴Truly I tell you, he will put that one in charge of all his possessions. ⁴⁵But if that slave says to himself, "My master is delayed in coming", and if he begins to beat the other slaves, men and women, and to eat and drink and get drunk, ⁴⁶the master of that slave will come on a day when he does not expect him and at an hour that he does not know, and will cut him in pieces, and put him with the unfaithful. ⁴⁷That slave who knew what his master wanted, but did not prepare himself or do what was wanted, will receive a severe beating. ⁴⁸But one who did not know and did what deserved a beating will receive a light beating. From everyone to whom much has been given, much will be required; and from one to whom much has been entrusted, even more will be demanded. (NRSV)

27. The Traveling Owner Of The House

Mark 13:34-37

[34]It is like a man going on a journey, when he leaves home and puts his slaves in charge, each with his work, and commands the doorkeeper to be on the watch. [35]Therefore, keep awake—for you do not know when the master of the house will come, in the evening, or at midnight, or at cockcrow, or at dawn, [36]or else he may find you asleep when he comes suddenly. [37]And what I say to you I say to all: Keep awake.' (NRSV)

PARABLES OF JUDGMENT AND THE FUTURE
ABOUT GOD'S VALUES

28. The Two Sons
Matthew 21:28-32

28 'What do you think? A man had two sons; he went to the first and said, "Son, go and work in the vineyard today." ^{29}He answered, "I will not"; but later he changed his mind and went. ^{30}The father went to the second and said the same; and he answered, "I go, sir"; but he did not go. ^{31}Which of the two did the will of his father?' They said, 'The first.' Jesus said to them, 'Truly I tell you, the tax-collectors and the prostitutes are going into the kingdom of God ahead of you. ^{32}For John came to you in the way of righteousness and you did not believe him, but the tax-collectors and the prostitutes believed him; and even after you saw it, you did not change your minds and believe him. (NRSV)

29. The Wicked Tenants
Matthew 21:33, 34

33 'Listen to another parable. There was a landowner who planted a vineyard, put a fence around it, dug a wine press in it, and built a watch-tower. Then he leased it to tenants and went to another country. ^{34}When the harvest time had come, he sent his slaves to the tenants to collect his produce. (NRSV)

Mark 12:1-9	Luke 20:9-16
Then he began to speak to them in parables. 'A man planted a vineyard, put a fence around it, dug a pit for the wine press, and built a watch-tower; then he leased it to tenants and went to another country. [2]When the season came, he sent a slave to the tenants to collect from them his share of the produce of the vineyard. [3]But they seized him, and beat him, and sent him away empty-handed. [4]And again he sent another slave to them; this one they beat over the head and insulted. [5]Then he sent another, and that one they killed. And so it was with many others; some they beat, and others they killed. [6]He had still one other, a beloved son. Finally he sent him to them, saying, "They will respect my son." [7]But those tenants said to one another, "This is the heir; come, let us kill him, and the inheritance will be ours." [8]So they seized him, killed him, and threw him out of the vineyard. [9]What then will the owner of the vineyard do? He will come and destroy the tenants and give the vineyard to others. (NRSV)	9 He began to tell the people this parable: 'A man planted a vineyard, and leased it to tenants, and went to another country for a long time. [10]When the season came, he sent a slave to the tenants in order that they might give him his share of the produce of the vineyard; but the tenants beat him and sent him away empty-handed. [11]Next he sent another slave; that one also they beat and insulted and sent away empty-handed. [12]And he sent yet a third; this one also they wounded and threw out. [13]Then the owner of the vineyard said, "What shall I do? I will send my beloved son; perhaps they will respect him." [14]But when the tenants saw him, they discussed it among themselves and said, "This is the heir; let us kill him so that the inheritance may be ours." [15]So they threw him out of the vineyard and killed him. What then will the owner of the vineyard do to them? [16]He will come and destroy those tenants and give the vineyard to others.' When they heard this, they said, 'Heaven forbid!' (NRSV)

83

30. The Unproductive Fig Tree

Luke 13:6-9

6 Then he told this parable: 'A man had a fig tree planted in his vineyard; and he came looking for fruit on it and found none. [7]So he said to the gardener, "See here! For three years I have come looking for fruit on this fig tree, and still I find none. Cut it down! Why should it be wasting the soil?" [8]He replied, "Sir, let it alone for one more year, until I dig round it and put manure on it. [9]If it bears fruit next year, well and good; but if not, you can cut it down." ' (NRSV)

31. The Marriage Feast

Matthew 22:1-14

Once more Jesus spoke to them in parables, saying: [2]'The kingdom of heaven may be compared to a king who gave a wedding banquet for his son. [3]He sent his slaves to call those who had been invited to the wedding banquet, but they would not come. [4]Again he sent other slaves, saying, "Tell those who have been invited: Look, I have prepared my dinner, my oxen and my fat calves have been slaughtered, and everything is ready; come to the wedding banquet." [5]But they made light of it and went away, one to his farm, another to his business, [6]while the rest seized his slaves, maltreated them, and killed them. [7]The king was enraged. He sent his troops, destroyed those murderers, and burned their city. [8]Then he said to his slaves, "The wedding is ready, but those invited were not worthy. [9]Go therefore into the main streets, and invite everyone you find to the wedding banquet." [10]Those slaves went out into the streets and gathered all whom they found, both good and bad; so the wedding hall was filled with guests.

11 'But when the king came in to see the guests, he noticed a man there who was not wearing a wedding robe, [12]and he said to him, "Friend, how did you get in here without a wedding robe?" And he was speechless. [13]Then the king said to the attendants, "Bind him hand and foot, and throw him into the outer darkness, where there will be weeping and gnashing of teeth." [14]For many are called, but few are chosen.' (NRSV)

32. The Unforgiving Servant

Matthew 18:23-25

23 'For this reason the kingdom of heaven may be compared to a king who wished to settle accounts with his slaves. [24]When he began the reckoning, one who owed him ten thousand talents* was brought to him; [25]and, as he could not pay, his lord ordered him to be sold, together with his wife and children and all his possessions, and payment to be made. (NRSV)

Made in the USA
Middletown, DE
29 September 2016